Dancing on the Farm

AF207209

by Jean Groce

Printed in the United States of America

ISBN 0-15-313853-X

Ordering Options
ISBN 0-15-313991-9 (Grade 1 Collection)
ISBN 0-15-314062-3 (package of 5)

2 3 4 5 6 7 8 9 10 026 99

I like to ask Dad about what he did when he was a boy. He can make up a great story!

One day we were working together. "Dad, did you have to work when you were little?" Brad asked.

1

Dad stopped working and sat down on the step.

"Did I have to work!" he said. "Every day I started working right after breakfast. I didn't stop until it was time for dinner!"

"What did you do?" I asked.

"A little of this and a little of that," Dad said. "I took care of our animals in the morning."

"Do you mean you fed them?" asked Brad. "That isn't much work."

Dad said, "I fed them, but that wasn't all. I had to help with our dancing sheep, too. Now that was work!"

"Dancing sheep? You had dancing sheep?" I asked.

"Oh, yes," said Dad. "My mother liked to dance. She showed the sheep how to dance, too. Have you danced with sheep? It's fun. They always step on your feet."

"Why in the world did you want your sheep to dance?" asked Brad.

"To keep the goat happy," Dad said. "A goat that isn't happy is not very nice to have around."

Then Dad said,
"That goat was a pet.
Some goats make good
pets. All that goat made
was trouble. She walked
across the garden to eat
the plants. She ate the
hats right off our heads.
I felt like screaming the
day she kicked our car!"

5

My mother was getting mad. She said I had to find a way to make the goat stop doing all that.

I didn't know what to do. After some time, I sat down and had a chat with that goat.

"Goat, you are making big trouble." I said. "Why are you doing all this?"

The goat stopped eating my mother's scarf. "It's like this," she said. "This place isn't much fun. What can a goat do all day but nap and eat? We goats need our fun, right?"

I had to say the goat was right, so
I asked, "What do you want to do?"
"Dance," said the goat.
"Dance?" I asked.
"Yes, dance," said the goat.
"Dancing is fun."

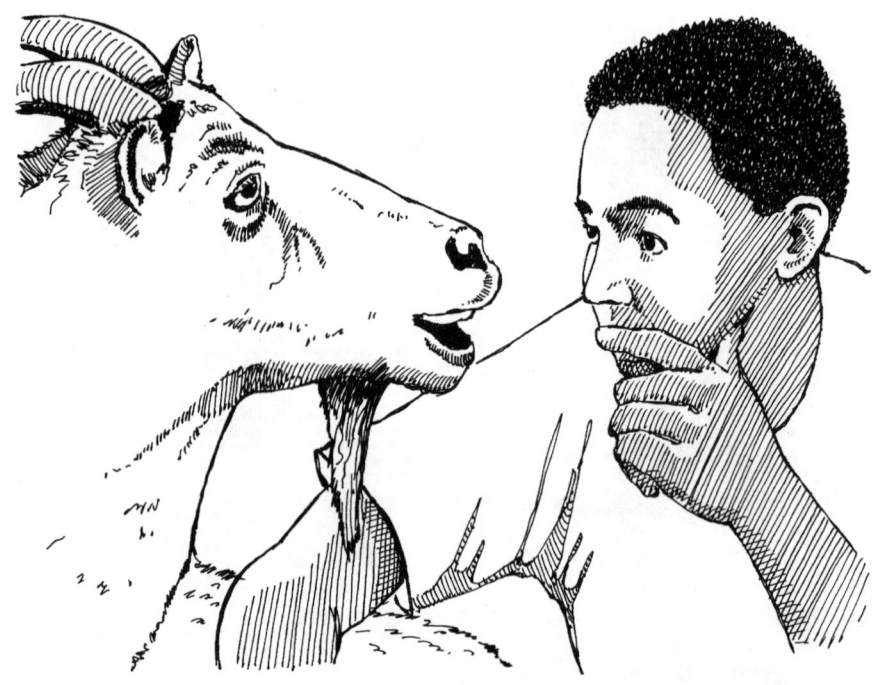

"Who will dance
with you?" I asked.
"You are the only goat
we have."

"I wish you would dance
with me," said the goat.

"No!" I snapped. "I am
not going to dance with a goat!"

"Maybe the sheep, then," the goat
said. "Your mother can show them
how to dance. Then when they are
dancing, I'll just jump right in."

9

That very day my mother took the sheep out behind the house. She showed them some dance steps. It took a while, and I had to help. Before night came, the sheep were dancing!

The goat came over to watch. Soon she was dancing right along with the sheep. She looked very happy. From that day on, she and the sheep danced every day. She never did eat up the garden or kick the car again.

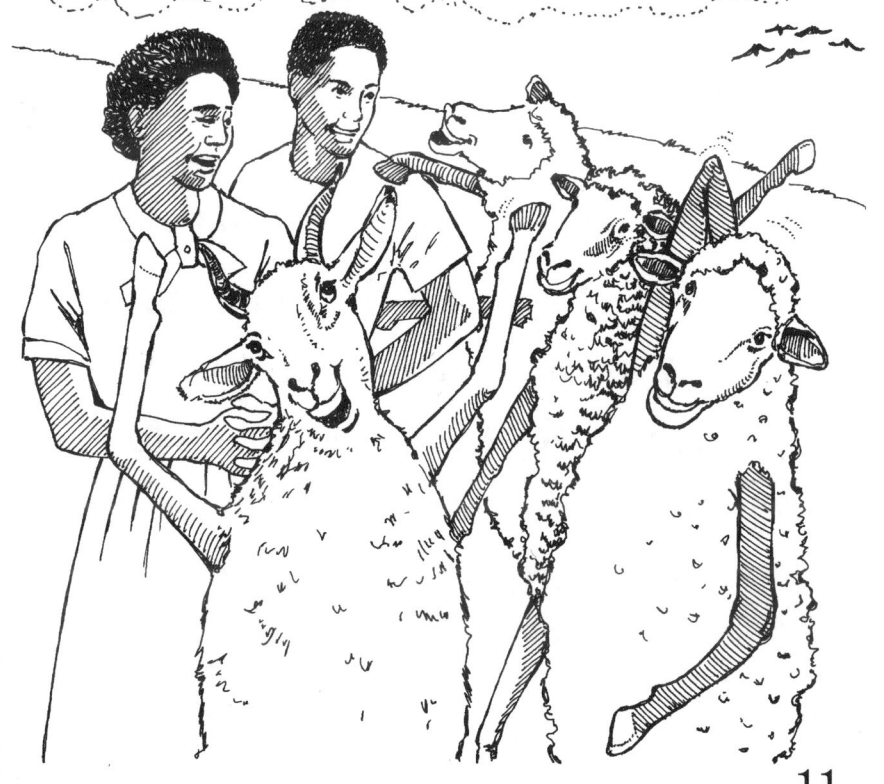

"The goat was happy, so that
story had a happy ending, Dad," I said.

"It was happy for the goat, but not
so happy for me," said Dad. "Every
day I had to work with the sheep to
keep them dancing. That's why I think
the work we are doing is not so bad.
It isn't as much work as dancing with
sheep!"

12

TAKE-HOME BOOK

All Smiles

Use with "Geraldine's Baby Brother."